TABLE OF CONTENTS

Introduction 6

Early Navajo Jewelry 8

Contemporary Navajo Jewelry 10

Cast Work.....................................12

Hand Hammered and Stamped 14

Repousse 16

Applique 18

Early Zuni Jewelry 20

Contemporary Zuni Jewelry 22

Clusterwork 24

Mosaic Inlay 26

Channel Inlay 28

Fetish Jewelry 30

Early Hopi Jewelry 32

Contemporary Hopi Jewelry 34

Overlay 36

Mosaic Inlay 38

Santo Domingo Jewelry...................40

Stone and Shell Beadwork 42

Mosaic Inlay 44

Glossary 46

INTRODUCTION

The foundation of Indian jewelry today by Navajo,
Zuni, Hopi, and Santo Domingo artists in
many ways links to centuries of jewelry work
in the Southwest.

Long before silver appeared in the area, stones such
as turquoise and shells—traded into the area—
comprised the core materials for jewelry work.
In the 1920s Neil Judd, curator of archeology for
the United States National Museum (now part
of the Smithsonian) uncovered a four-strand,
2,500-bead turquoise necklace at Chaco Culture
National Historical Park. The beauty of the piece
impressed Judd for the rest of his life.

The descendents of the people who created this early
piece—and others like it—now reside in villages
along the Rio Grande in New Mexico; the village
of Zuni, New Mexico; and the mesas of the Hopi
Nation in Arizona.

Later arrivals to the Southwest, the Navajo played an
integral role in the transformation of Indian jewelry
by learning silverworking techniques in the 1850s,
which they subsequently passed on to the Zuni and
Hopi people.

Today, greater varieties of metals and stones have
increased the possible styles and interpretations of

earlier work. Silversmiths use materials from all over the world, though the most coveted turquoise continues to come from mines in the Southwest. Artists also use quality Chinese and Persian turquoise because of the accessibility of these stones. Other stones frequently found in contemporary Indian jewelry include lapis lazuli and *charoite*.

Albert Banteah, 1997, pendant

Whether you buy from artists or dealers, be certain of their reputation. Make sure they guarantee their work. Unfortunately, imitations have flooded the Indian art market. Ask questions. When making a purchase, ask for a certificate of authenticity. An honest artist or dealer will put it in writing.

Most important, keep an open mind. Indian jewelry, like any artwork, is subjective. If you see a piece you like, buy it. Just as each piece expresses the individuality of the artist who created it, so does it express the individuality of the person who wears it.

Italicized terms are explained in the Glossary, page 46.

EARLY NAVAJO JEWELRY

A Mexican man living near Mt. Taylor, New Mexico,
around 1850 first introduced blacksmithing to a
Navajo man, Atsidi Sani ("Old Smith"). It is not
clear if Atsidi Sani was the first Navajo metal-
worker, but he was certainly the most prominent
of his time. After returning from the Navajo's
internment at Fort Sumner in New Mexico and
the Long Walk in 1868, Atsidi Sani started working
with silver. He taught his four sons, who in turn
taught others on the newly formed Navajo Nation.

Early jewelry pieces consisted of simple earrings,
ketohs (bowguards), belt fasteners, and bracelets.

Traders provided tools and supplies such as silver
coins and *slugs*. More important, traders gave
Indian silversmiths a place to trade and sell their
work. In the 1920s, sheet silver replaced silver
slugs, allowing artists to work more quickly since
they no longer needed to melt and pound the
slugs flat. A Navajo style evolved, typified by heavy
silverwork, sometimes worked around stones.

Artist unknown, bowguard

CONTEMPORARY NAVAJO JEWELRY

Using a number of techniques, contemporary Navajo artists continue to focus on hammering, bending, and molding metals. Artists choose shapes and designs that display the natural beauty of metals such as silver, gold, and platinum.

Other enhancements to pieces include permanent darkening through *oxidation* or texturing to create a variety of surfaces. Stonework has shifted to become the focal point of many pieces by Navajo artists.

Dorothy Small Canyon, 1998, squashblossom necklace

CAST WORK

One early technique still used by Navajo silversmiths
is making silver castings in sand or stone molds.
The artist carves a design into damp sand or tuff—
a porous volcanic stone—and then secures a second
flat stone on top to complete the mold. Using a
crucible, he or she then pours melted silver into
the mold through a carved channel. Air vents allow
steam to escape, preventing air bubbles from
forming in the cooling silver.

After the silver has cooled and hardened, the artist
removes the piece from the mold. Any silver not
part of the overall design is cut off and the edges
are filed smooth. All surfaces of the jewelry are
ground and polished. Sometimes, artists add
stones as a final accent.

Artist unknown, belt buckle

HAND HAMMERED AND STAMPED

Early silversmithing originated from blacksmithing
techniques that required the heating and softening
of metal interspersed with hammering to work the
metal into desired shapes. Great skill is required
to balance these opposite forces. Too much heating and hammering causes the piece to become
"work-hardened" and it may become brittle and
crack. Too little force can lead to a poorly shaped
piece with shallow, inconsistent design work.

After shaping the piece, the silversmith uses a *graver*
or *die* stamps to inscribe designs into the metal.
Many artists create their own carved metal stamps
to add design elements such as lines or swirls to
their jewelry. The artist places the designed end
on the desired spot of the jewelry piece then
strikes, stamping the design into the metal surface.
A good silversmith strikes the stamp evenly each
time, producing a consistent design.

Perry Shorty, 1998, concha belt

REPOUSSE

A variation on the hand-stamping technique,
repousse consists of designs raised in the silver.
At first glance, this style may seem simple, but
it can prove to be very challenging.

To create the raised design, the artist first stamps a
design into the underside of a piece of jewelry,
which raises a design on the front. If stamped too
lightly, the pattern will not be sufficiently raised
and if he or she stamps too hard or too often,
the artist runs the risk of making the silver brittle.
For pieces including more than one design
element, the artist must stamp with uniform
pressure. After the design has been raised from
the back, the artist turns the piece to the front
and may create a contrasting surface by incising
an outline, stamping some additional designs,
or using some other technique such as oxidation
or texturing.

Harry Morgan, 1998, belt buckle

APPLIQUE

Applique, which is often identified with Navajo silver-
    work, includes shapes such as leaves, feathers, and
    flowers cut from sheet or wire silver and then
    soldered onto an underlying piece. Artists may also
    twist the wire into various forms and attach them
    as decoration. One contemporary adaptation in
    this style includes jewelry appliqued with gold
    rather than silver.

Leo Francis, 1998, bracelet

EARLY ZUNI JEWELRY

The Zuni and their ancestors have created jewelry for more than one thousand years. Jewelry found at the ancestral Zuni dwelling of Hawikuh includes inlaid animal pendants and wooden combs featuring many tiny pieces of jet and turquoise grouped together. This early tendency toward stonework remains a signature of Zuni jewelry.

The Zuni people learned silversmithing from the Navajo sometime in the early 1870s. Anthropologist John Adair visited Zuni in 1937 and 1938. He interviewed the Pueblo's first silversmith, La:niyadhi. According to those interviews, Atsidi Chon ("Ugly Smith"), a Navajo silversmith who was a friend and trading partner of La:niyadhi, moved to Zuni. Atsidi Chon made jewelry for the Zuni people but kept his techniques to himself. Finally—for the payment of a horse—Atsidi Chon taught La:niyahdi to make iron stamps and decorate silver. La:niyahdi eventually taught other men at Zuni.

Artist unknown, 1940s, cluster squashblossom necklace

CONTEMPORARY ZUNI JEWELRY

The foundation laid by the early silversmiths at Zuni led to a style that puts great emphasis on stone-work. Pieces often incorporate many stones assembled to form an intricate design and visually pleasing piece.

Since it is a small community, these artists are very much aware of other artists' work, and carefully create their own styles. Often families become known for distinct styles.

Amy Wesley, 1998, bracelet

CLUSTERWORK

In the early days, Navajo and Zuni silver jewelry
looked very similar. However, intricate stonework,
such as clusterwork, combined with silverwork
gradually became the basis for contemporary Zuni
design. Clusterwork consists of well-matched
stones or shell arranged into flower-like patterns
known as "clusters." Petitpoint and needlepoint
techniques are a refinement of this cluster technique. Petitpoint consists of small stones rounded
on one side, using a grinding wheel to create a
teardrop-like shape. Needlepoint stones are
shaped with points on both ends.

Artist unknown, 1940s, needlepoint squashblossom necklace

MOSAIC INLAY

The discovery of prehistoric jewelry at the ancient village of Hawikuh inspired a revival of mosaic work in the 1920s. The updated technique utilized silver backing rather than wood.

Modern mosaic work features an array of stones and shell from around the world. The artist designs the overall form and then individually cuts each stone to fit tightly with the other stones in the piece.

Another type of mosaic work, called overlay inlay, features two pieces of silver, one for the backing and the second, with a pattern cut from the silver, soldered on top. Rather than leaving the silver empty as in Hopi overlay, Zuni artists fill the opening with stones "laid in" to form a mosaic design.

Artist unknown, 1938, pin

CHANNEL INLAY

Channel inlay is a variation of mosaic inlay. The
artist creates soldered silver compartments within
the backing. Cut stones, such as turquoise, fitted
within the compartments create repetitive geometric designs or figurative pieces. The compartments strengthen the integrity of the many
stones within a mosaic piece and provide an
added design element.

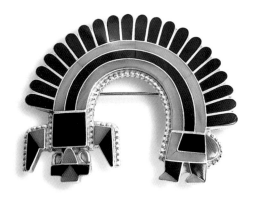

Fadrian Bowannie, 1997, pin

FETISH JEWELRY

Since ancient times, the Pueblo people have used
fetish carvings for protection and blessings.
Originally carved from stones found near the
pueblo or from traded shells, early fetish jewelry
consisted of simple stone-and-shell necklaces,
which might contain several animal fetishes or
a single animal pendant.

Fetish carvings still figure strongly in a Pueblo artist's
life and livelihood as well as serving as design
elements in their jewelry. The variety of materials
and originality of carvings have made Zuni fetish
jewelry popular.

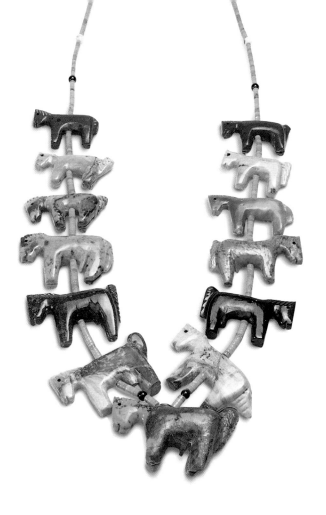

Ellen Quandelacy, 1994, necklace

EARLY HOPI JEWELRY

The Hopi have lived in many of their villages since at least the 1500s, occupying some sites since the 1100s. Early jewelry consisted of mosaic inlay and beadwork created from stones, shells, wood, bones, and seeds.

The Zuni silversmith La:niyadhi was also responsible for carrying the techniques to the Hopi Pueblos. La:niyadhi passed along his knowledge of silverwork to a Hopi man named Sikyatala ("Yellow Light"). After acquiring tools and a *forge*, Sikyatala was able to produce pieces needed at that time, such as concha belts and bowguards. By 1906 silversmiths were working at all the Hopi mesas.

The styles made from 1900 to 1940 were similar to silver jewelry made by Navajo and Zuni silversmiths during the same period. Dr. Harold S. Colton and his wife, Mary-Russell Ferrell Colton, founders of the Museum of Northern Arizona, had an early impact on Hopi crafts. They suggested applying Hopi pottery, basketry, and textile designs to the jewelry for a unique style.

Artist unknown, 1930s, bolo tie

CONTEMPORARY HOPI JEWELRY

After World War II, a training program featured an eighteen-month silversmithing course for returning Hopi servicemen. Paul Saufkie served as technical instructor and Fred Kabotie taught design. The two teachers used a book of *Mimbres* designs put together by Kabotie to augment Hopi designs used at the time. These designs continue to inspire many elements used in today's Hopi jewelry.

Phillip Secakuku, 1998, bolo tie

OVERLAY

Overlay evolved from the applique techniques originally suggested by founders of the Museum of
Northern Arizona. This style includes a background soldered to another like-sized piece with
a cutout design. The silver background is then
oxidized and often scratched or stamped to bring
out a contrast between the two pieces. Silversmiths
often work in both overlay and applique to avoid
wasting silver. Today, some artists use combina-
tions of gold and silver, though most artists continue to use silver for the backdrop piece, as it
provides a strong contrast to gold.

Phillip Weseoma, 1999, bracelet

MOSAIC INLAY

The greatest shift in contemporary Hopi jewelry came
through the work of Charles Loloma, a versatile
artist from Hotevilla. In 1950, while living at
Shungopavi, Loloma became interested in silverwork. During this period, many Hopi men con-
tinued to work in the ancient mosaic inlay style.
In 1972, Loloma did a unique interpretation.
Using mosaic inlay to line the inside of one of his
gold bracelets, he placed stonework against the
wearer's skin and therefore invisible to the casual
observer. His influence opened the door for new
interpretations of silver and gold jewelry.

Sherian Honhongra, 1999, belt buckle

SANTO DOMINGO JEWELRY

While contemporary Indian jewelry has followed many paths, the work most closely linked to the work of ancestral Puebloans is the stone and shell work produced at Santo Domingo Pueblo in New Mexico.

When stone merchants come to the village, competition for turquoise and other materials is fierce. Using five-gallon cans for chairs, women arrange themselves around a table piled with turquoise to individually pick stones they will use in their work. Artists also look for coral and shell without holes and of uniform color.

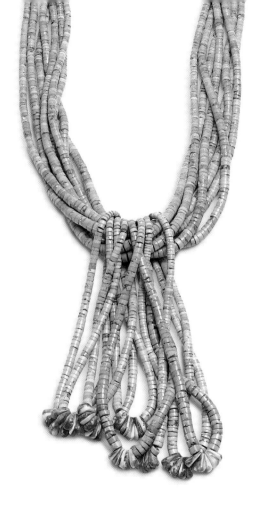

Ray Lovato, 1998, necklace

STONE AND SHELL BEADWORK

For this work (known as *discoidal* beadwork) rough-cut stones are first drilled—usually with electric drills and grinding machines—and then strung on a wire. Next the artist holds both ends of a strand and carefully draws the beads back and forth across a grinding wheel or other rough surface, shaping the *heishi*. The diameter of the beads can be very fine or more substantial. The artist then strings the beads on a softer material, such as cotton. The beads should feel uniform and smooth to the touch.

Unfortunately, some stone merchants provide polished and drilled stones with foreign-made shell heishi for stringing. The unscrupulous will simply string these materials and offer the result as authentic handmade pieces. Beware of necklaces where beads do not fit into each other and feel rough when you run your hands down the string of disks. They do not demonstrate the fit of a proper Santo Domingo necklace.

Joe Tortalita, 1998, necklace

MOSAIC INLAY

Mosaic inlay is still prevalent among several families
at Santo Domingo Pueblo. Traditional backings—
wood or shell—gave way to experimental materials
such as phonograph records or car batteries in the
early half of the twentieth century. Today shell is
widely used as backing. Artists may leave the shells
in their natural form or trim them to a certain
shape. As with other mosaic inlay, the artist then
creates a design or pattern on the backing with
many varied-sized stones. Santo Domingo mosaic
work tends to be more abstract in design than the
geometric and pictorial mosaics of Zuni artists.

Artist unknown, 1930s, necklace

GLOSSARY

Charoite: A purple stone discovered in Russia in 1978 and named for the Charo River near where it was found.

Die: Various tools or devices for imparting a desired shape, form, or finish to a material.

Discoidal: Resembling or producing a disk.

Fetish: An object believed to have magical power to protect or aid its owner.

Forge: A furnace where metal is heated and wrought.

Graver: Any of a variety of cutting or shaving tools used in engraving or in hand metal-turning.

Heishi: A Santo Domingo word for shells, used in broad terms to describe discoidal jewerly.

Mimbres: A regional group of the Mogollon culture occupying villages in southwestern New Mexico until approximately A.D. 1200.

Oxidation: A chemical process that blackens silver.

Slugs: Pieces of silver roughly shaped for processing by a silversmith.

Solder: A metal or metallic alloy used when melted to join metallic surfaces.